GOODNIGHT HOMEROOM

All the Advice I Wish I Got Before Going to High School

SAM KAPLAN & KEITH RIEGERT

illustrated by EMILY FROMM

ULYSSES PRESS

Published by:
Ulysses Press
PO Box 3440
Berkeley, CA 94703
www.ulyssespress.com

ISBN: 978-1-64604-455-9

Printed in China
10 9 8 7 6 5 4 3 2 1

Three years just went by
in the blink of an eye.
Now you're 13 (or 14)—
let out one big sigh!

Sixth grade was a blast.
Year seven was sweet.
And year eight was so great!
Middle school is complete.

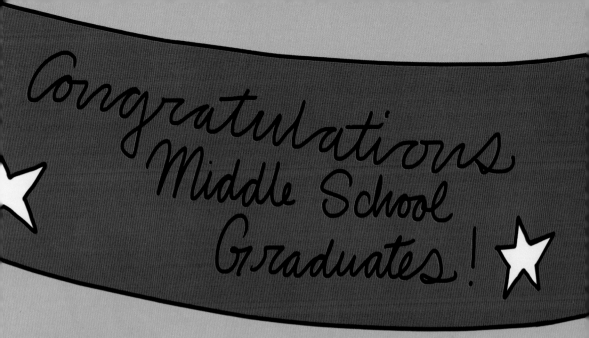

Congratulations
Middle School
Graduates!

You survived all your classes,
made a fun group of friends.
Graduation is here!
Is this really the end?

But with each certain end
comes the freshest of starts.
Here are guidelines for high school,
the best of life's parts!

The first piece of wisdom
we'll bring to your senses
relates to the summer
before high school commences:

Make the most of these days
with your middle school crew,
'cause when you next see them
you'll be differently new.

You will each have
a new school to attend,
classes to master,
and new pals to befriend.

So savor these moments
before your goodbyes.
Next time you meet, you'll feel
more grown-up inside.

Sometime this summer
comes a blip in vacation
when you're pressed to get dressed
for . . . high school orientation!

Here's where you learn
how to navigate school—
to zip through your schedule and
maintain your cool.

You'll learn all the rules
and which classes to take,
then ask pressing questions
like, "What time is break?"

Here's also your chance
to meet some new chums
to lessen your stressin'
when that first day comes.

ENGLISH L

The sun's getting lower
and summer is fading.
This is the Big Day
for which you've been waiting!

You're a freshman! A noob!
Your heart will be thumping.
The first day of high school
Will get your nerves jumping.

Just remember this thought
As you hop on the bus:
All freshmen are newbies.
You ALL have to adjust.

So approach it with glee,
but don't rush too quickly.
This is only day one
of fourteen hundred and sixty!
(plus or minus)

Be you a goth,
a floater, or jock,
or a hipster obsessed
with shojo or Crocs...

Or be you a fully
star-struck drama nerd
just be you! You don't need . . .
to be part of a herd!

Don't let the trends trick you
or stick you in a box.
You're the bomb as you are
You're a stone-cold boss fox.

You've learned this before.
You may need a refresher.
It won't ever pay
To give in to peer pressure.

There's one part of high school
that's perhaps the most messy:
That's finding your people
and making a bestie.

Be patient! Slow down!
Act polite and sincere.
If you're open and kind,
your new crew will appear.

And maybe you've heard
about bullies and hazing
and seniors who try
to make life less amazing.

Stay calm and stay strong.
Don't you rise to the bait.
Laugh off what they're saying;
walk away from the hate.

Soon comes the time
to try out for some sports
like quidditch or peezeball
or pong played with sporks.

Or maybe your thing's
not a team but a club
like coding or theater
or Bubs Who Love Shrubs.

There are affinity groups!
And robotics! And dance!
Be brave. Go to tryouts!
They're well worth the chance!

'Cause extracurriculars
may look great on your apps,
but they're another chance
to meet amazing new chaps.

There's a week in the fall
when high school starts a-humming,
'cause students are returning
for the yearly homecoming.

Classes basically stop
so each grade can compete
in contests of spirit.
You best not get beat!

5

It'll seem like your school's
spared zero finances
for parades and pep rallies
and homecoming dances.

And in a tradition
that may tickle your spleen,
you might be selected
as king or as queen.

Now comes the part
when we talk about hearts
and the way they can swell
or get broken apart.

First comes the phase
where your cheeks start to blush
and your words turn to mush—
you've just met your first crush!

In the blink of an eye,
you heart is pulsating
because your big crush
is now someone you're dating!

But alas, we must warn you:
Please make no mistake.
There's no way to avoid
your first big heartbreak.

Feel all of your feelings,
and swallow your pride.
But your studies await.
Take emotions in stride.

School doesn't come
to a stop 'cause you're hurting.
There are quizzes and tests—
you're constantly learning

A difference between
upper school and the middle
is teachers won't coddle you
like when you're little.

It may feel just great
to have new independence,
but aim to achieve
more than perfect attendance.

What we're trying to say
in our long-winded way
is that you must STUDY.
Make haste! Don't delay!

Find a stump for your rump
that is quiet and quaint
or a four-person hammock
that bridges the lake.

For the hardest tests,
study with more than one smarty
and mash up your brains
at a studying party.

(When picking the buddies
with whom you will study,
choose folks who are focused,
or your grades will get crummy.)

We don't mean to pry
and we don't mean to pester,
but have you prepared
for the end of semester?

Pressure's built up
and your tensions have festered,
so we hope you've become
the most bestest of testers.

Because this time of the year
boils down to survival
and making it through
about two trillion finals.

So sketch out your schedule
for every exam,
and space out your studies
so you don't have to cram.

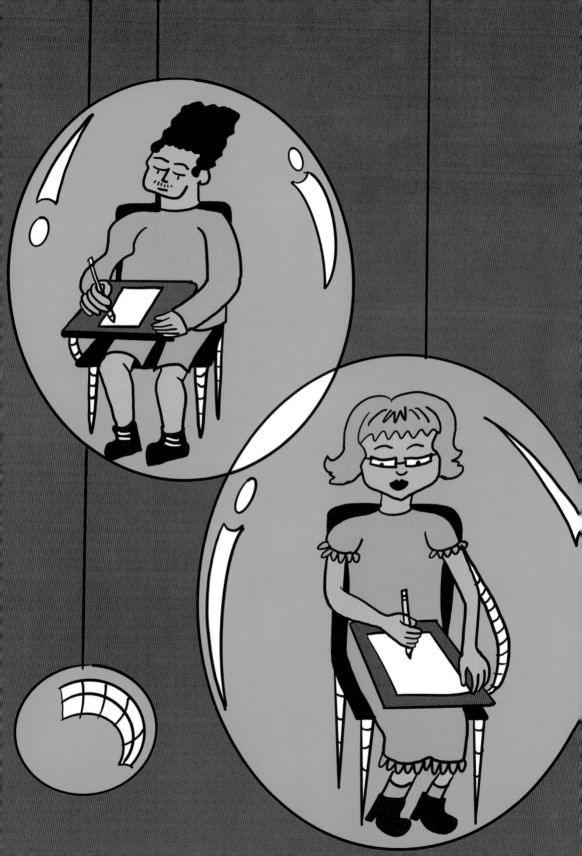

You may have forgotten
about your new biffles
between all your tests
and your panicky sniffles.

But exam week is over!
You're done! You survived!
Now you get to let loose
Until you're revived.

So hit up your homies
and try to remember
there's nothing quite like
winter break in December.

Make the most of these days.
They'll pass by in a flash!
Then it's back to the hustle.
Get your butt back to class!

The second semester
of your freshman year
went by in a breeze.
Now year two is here!

You're a sophomore! Tenth grader!
No longer fresh meat!
You've earned more respect,
and you've grown to twelve feet.

It feels splendidly fine
to climb social ladders.
But with advancement comes
tougher subject matter.

There's chemistry! Government!
Algebra One squared by two.
The teachers are tough.
Will you make it through?

Just when you've found
your feet firm on the ground,
there's a new task to master:
how to drive safe and sound.

Before cruising around
having fun, look ahead:
You must first make it through
dull days of driver's ed.

A permit permits you
to drive with your parent.
But remember at first
that your skills will be errant.

So listen! And practice!
And don't be so hasty.
Abide by the law;
there's always time for safety.

You've probably noticed
the forming of groups,
from the punks with blue mohawks
to the jocks who shoot hoops.

There are gymnasts and brainiacs,
band geeks and loners,
emos and hippies,
romantics and roamers.

They can be quite exclusive,
but once you are in,
these groups will begin
to feel just like your kin.

But don't close yourself off
to folks outside your clique.
Keep your heart open wide,
and don't ever be a . . . jerk.

One fun part of high school
where you'll be selective
is choosing a few
of your favorite electives.

You'll be most effective
in subjects you know,
but to change your perspective
may be how you grow.

So try dancing! Or drama!
Or graphic design!
Or even a class called
Canning Pickles in Brine.

And while you are trying
to find your true purpose,
don't forget to give back
with community service.

The day's finally here!
It could not have come sooner.
Grade eleven is heaven!
You're a big dawg—a junior.

But slow down your roll
and reign in your horses,
'cause this year has the toughest,
most torturous courses.

There are pre-calc and physics
and advanced-placement history,
and the answers to quizzes
are shrouded in mystery.

The teachers are stricter,
but we know you'll survive.
Put your nose to the grindstone,
and surely you'll thrive!

Somewhere between,
all your studies and fretting,
may seem there's something
quite big you're forgetting.

We got you!
It's why you are reading this book!
That thing you're forgetting?
It's college! Go look!

First make a list
of your very top choices.
Get a feel for the vibe;
they've got unique "voices."

And when you are ready,
strike out on a tour
in search of a match
that you love to your core.

Ugh! Oh my gosh!
Geewillickers! Fuddle!
It feels like your brain's
on the floor in a puddle.

On top of your classwork,
you must be prepared:
College entrance exams
leave some students quite scared.

SATs! ACTs!
Subject tests! O-M-G.
With all of these acronyms,
will you ever be free?

But this, too, shall pass.
And so, too, shall you.
Stay focused, keep going,
and you'll make it through.

As your stressors and struggles
start making things rough,
soon you'll discover
that you're really tough.

You've got this! We promise!
You're quite an achiever!
You've turned your inner doubter
to fervent believer.

You may feel compelled
to take every tough class.
But that's a surefire way
to fall flat on your. . . face.

Pick APs and honors
with extra strong caution.
And take mental health breaks
not sometimes, but often.

At some point this year,
you'll find you're in a slump—
academically fried,
and you also got dumped.

With your head- and heartaches,
your angst has compounded.
So you stayed out past curfew
and then found yourself grounded.

Try your best not to spiral.
Don't let yourself stew.
This phase—it won't last.
It's just junior-year blues.

Keep your head on your shoulders
and your feet in your socks.
If you practice self-care,
you'll get past all these knocks.

YEAR

Oh triumph! What beauty!
What glorious glory!
You're finally a senior!
Near the end of your story!

The peons beneath you
will cower in fear:
You're the biggest of bigshots
on campus this year.

Class is a breeze.
Your apps were so awesome!
Now's your chance to lead
and to help your school blossom.

So don't be a snot.
Use your powers for good!
And leave a great legacy
like you know you should.

The hardest part
of the hard parts of this year
is choosing your path
when the future's unclear.

University? Gap year?
Or learning a trade?
Make sure cons and pros
have been properly weighed.

It's true that you've come
to a fork in the road.
But mentors and advisors
can lighten that load.

Explore all your options
and think it all through.
Just make sure your choice
is the best choice for you.

March and April this year
can make your mood swing,
'cause letters from colleges
can come with a sting.

You may find you're engaging
in unhealthy dwelling,
awaiting to see
what the next email is telling.

But hold to your dreams.
You'll open it soon:
that one "yes" that matters.
You'll be over the moon!

And remember that college
is more than its name.
It's what you do there
that will bring you acclaim.

You're looking so neat-o!
You're looking the best
in a spiffy tuxedo!
Hey, a nice wallflower-print dress!

We hope that you wore
your best dancing footwear
'cause this evening will be
a most raucous affair!

The
S.S.
Senio

Whether you're dressed to impress
or dressed to express,
just remember this night's
one you'll never forget.

Try out your best dance moves
at your senior prom.
You're sure to have fun.
It will just be the bomb!

Prom

Four years from today
you'll be back in a cap.
You'll receive your diploma.
High school's now a wrap!

This here is your moment,
so savor it sweetly.
Reflect on your journey.
You've done it completely!

You've made true companions.
You've learned how to drive.
We've watched your brain growing.
It's tripled in size!

You've conquered your classes
and silenced the doubters.
What's next, now? The world!
We couldn't be prouder.

At first glance, your grad night
can feel like a dud.
But embrace it; don't waste it.
It's a night with your buds.

And with your classmates
you've been through thick and thin.
Together four years now!
You're basically kin.

Be present and kind.
Make the most of this moment.
The night will be over
'fore you even know it.

Yes, now is the the time
for your one last goodbye.
You'll feel bittersweet
(and you'll probably cry).

Another September
you'll pack up.
Your fam will feel proud
but incredibly sad.

You'll go across the country
(or just down the street).
New adventures to claim!
New besties to meet!

Your teen years will close
with a startling result:
you'll be solidly you
and a full-fledged adult.

That summer before high school?
Just a long-ago dream.
Your new life's a river,
not that childhood stream.

But not yet, our dear friend.
No, not yet, indeed.
You're just at the start,
and you're gathering speed.

As parts of life go,
there's just nothing better.
But when high school is gone,
it's gone, then—forever.

Yes, these most precious years
will zip by in a haze,
but your memories and friendships
will last all of your days.

So take a deep breath,
and wide-open your eyes,
'cause high school is your time,
and it's your time to rise.

ABOUT THE AUTHORS

Sam Kaplan studied psychology and balanced his studies by captaining his intramural soccer team, making didgeridoos, bowling every Thursday, and going on awesome road trips over the breaks. He is currently working toward his doctorate in clinical psychology. Sam lives in Oakland, California.

Keith Riegert read Kafka, Milton, and Joyce as a Creative Studies Literature major and surfed, painted, and lounged at UCSB. Keith lives in New York.

Sam and Keith are the authors of *The MANual*, *Going Ninja*, and *When Ninjas Attack*.

ABOUT THE ILLUSTRATOR

Emily Fromm earned a bachelor of arts degree from San Francisco State University in studio art, with emphases in painting, drawing, and ceramics. When outside, she dabbled in ballet and biology and hung out at Ocean Beach. She is currently an active illustrator, visual artist, muralist, and designer in San Francisco, California.